FUNDAMENTAL PHONICS

By
Renee Cummings
and
Meish Goldish

Cover Artist
Mia Tavonatti

Inside Illustrations by
Becky Radtke

Publisher
Instructional Fair • TS Denison
Grand Rapids, Michigan 49544

Permission to Reproduce

About the Book

The *"Fun"damental Phonics* series was developed to incorporate language fun into phonics learning. The extensive use of poetry throughout the series is based on the premise that rhyme is one of the best tools to help students find patterns as they learn new sounds and words.

About the Authors

Renee Cummings brings 18 years of classroom experience to the books she has authored for teachers and children. Her other titles for Ideal • Instructional Fair include *Literature-Based Reading* and *Reading Comprehension*. Renee lives in Hood River, Oregon, with her husband, who is currently the town's mayor.

Meish Goldish has written more than 30 books for children, in a range that includes fiction, nonfiction, biography, and several poetry anthologies. His delightful phonics poems, found throughout this series, are his first works for Instructional Fair. Meish lives in Teaneck, New Jersey.

Credits

Authors: Renee Cummings and Meish Goldish
Cover Artist: Mia Tavonatti
Inside Illustrations: Becky Radtke
Project Director/Editor: Kathryn Wheeler
Editors: Sharon Kirkwood, Wendy Roh Jenks, Linda Kimble
Page Design: Pat Geasler

Standard Book Number: 1-56822-855-4
"Fun"damental Phonics—Grade 1
Copyright © 1999 Ideal • Instructional Fair Publishing Group
a division of Tribune Education
2400 Turner Avenue NW
Grand Rapids, Michigan 49544

Table of Contents

IF87101 "Fun"damental Phonics

Introduction

"Fun"damental Phonics is designed to engage students actively in language play as they listen to and recognize sounds. The poems, games, and writing activities will help students understand the relationship between letters and sounds. Elements of language acquisition include listening, speaking, reading, and writing. Teachers can informally assess learning while introducing, practicing, and reviewing initial and ending consonants; short and long vowels; and phonograms (word families).

The letters covered in this book are divided into consonants and vowels and then arranged alphabetically; however,

many teachers prefer to begin with the initial consonants *s, m, l, f, r,* and *z,* since these sounds can be sustained without distortion. Next, it is beneficial to include short vowels *a* and *i,* followed by consonants such as *t* and *d.* This sequence allows the teacher and students to construct many words based on phonograms or word families, i.e., *at, mat, fat, rat.*

Another general sequence of consonant instruction is as follows:

b	m	r	s
t	g	p	n
h	f	d	c
l	j	k	w
y	z	v	q

Poetry Presentation

Each lesson begins with a poem which can be transferred to an overhead transparency, chart paper, or a pocket chart. Poems may also be laminated and attached to a magnetic board with magnetic tape.

Ask students to listen as you read the poem out loud. Depending on your methodology, you may wish to follow from left to right with your finger or a pointer stick as you read. Invite interaction with the letter being introduced by asking questions, such as, "What is the same about the words *princess* and *pretend*? Yes, they both begin with *pr.* And *pr* makes the sound /pr/." You may also wish to point to a word in the poem and offer information, such as, "This word is *tub.* It ends with the letter *b,* which sounds like /b/. Can you find another word that ends with that letter and sound?"

It is possible to alter the poems by substituting new rhyming words. Simply apply a self-adhesive note to cover the old word with the new one. Encourage class participation in reading out loud. Try choral-reading. Create actions to go with a specific poem and then teach them to another class.

Focus on a specific beginning or ending consonant sound, blend, or phonogram, and ask students to clap or make a specified motion each time they hear that sound while you read the poem out loud.

Encourage students to brainstorm a list of words which feature the designated sound. Illustrate or chart these words to use as writing prompts.

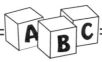

School-to-Home Connection

To keep parents/guardians informed of their child's progress in phonics learning, it would be helpful to send home the poem or worksheet of the week.

At the top of a page, place a blank line for the student's name followed by: "is learning about the letter (or phonogram) ____ and the sound it makes." Place the worksheet or other materials below this heading and attach it to a weekly newsletter explaining activities that took place in the classroom. This reinforces instruction about the featured letter.

On a designated day of the week, students might be asked to bring an object from home that begins with the featured letter. These objects can be used during group share time to facilitate discussion.

A variation of this activity would be to ask the student to find an item small enough to fit in a lunch bag. Then have him/her work at home to write three clues that describe the object. The teacher can help the student tell these clues to the class to see if the class can determine the mystery object.

Picture Cards

At the end of this book are pages of picture cards. These can be cut apart and laminated to use with individual students or small groups. They may also be used with an entire class if displayed on an overhead projector or magnetic board.

Several games can be played with the picture cards. They include:

Listen and Tell. Show a letter card for a beginning sound, ending sound, blend, or phonogram. Ask students to choose a picture to match the designated sound.

Concentration. Make a grid on a tabletop, mixing picture cards and cards with letters, blends, or phonograms. Turn up the cards one at a time. Have students make matches between the picture and the designated sound. Once a match has been made, leave the cards face up on the table. Continue until all pairs of cards are matched.

Sound Graphing. Make letter, blend, or phonogram cards for the headings of columns on a magnetic board. "Deal" the picture cards out to teams of students, and have them place pictures in the correct columns on the board. This game can be played relay-race style, or with individual players.

Bob's Bike

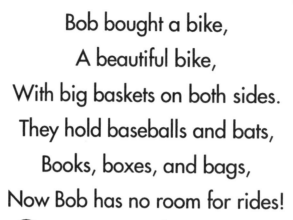

Bob bought a bike,
A beautiful bike,
With big baskets on both sides.
They hold baseballs and bats,
Books, boxes, and bags,
Now Bob has no room for rides!

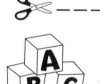

Come, Cozy Cat

Cute, cozy cat,
Curled up in a corner,
Care to come out for a break?
Cute, cozy cat,
I'm calling! Come!
In your cup is a cool carrot cake.

6

Dinner Dishes

Dinner is done,
The dishes are dirty,
Doing each dish is a chore!
Do be a dear
And help do the dishes—
Don't dare to dash out the door!

Foxy Fox

Foxy Fox found fifty figs
In a forest far away.
The figs were full,
The figs were fat,
The figs were falling,
Fancy that!

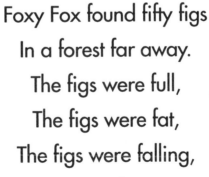

Goat and Goose A-Gobbling

Goat got the garbage
By the garage.
Goose got the goodies
By the garden gate.
Goat and Goose
Gobbled their goods
Before it was too late!

Helping Hands

Helping hands!
Hey! Hey, help!
Hurry to this hill!
I'm hanging here.
Please come near.
Grab my hand
And help me stand.

IF87101 "Fun"damental Phonics

Jeep Ride

Jungle-bumble jeep ride,

Jelly and jam,

Bounce with a jolt and a jeer.

Jam on my jacket!

Jelly on my jeans!

It's sticky and I can't steer!

Kangaroo Kick

Kangaroo, kick a kitchen sink,

Kick a kettle, a kite,

Or a key.

Kick a kerchief or a king,

Kick any kind of thing,

Kangaroo.

Just don't kick me!

IF87101 "Fun"damental Phonics

Library Lady

Library lady, look, look, look!
I'm looking for a library book.
Large or little, heavy or light,
I'm looking left and looking right!
Library lady, look, look, look!
Loan me a lovely library book.

Monday Morning March-Along

Monday morning,
Month of May,
Many mice march on their way
As Mister Mike milks the cow,
And Mister Cat moans, "Meow!"

Never a Noise

No one is here,
Nobody's near,
No nice neighbor next door.
Never a noise,
Nothing to notice,
Noon to night, what a bore!

Picnic in the Park

Picnic in the park,
Perfect sky,
Peanuts, popcorn,
Piece of pie!
Picnic in the park,
Pass the day,
Parties, a parade,
And pool play!

11

Quacking Queen Duck

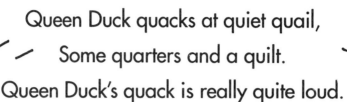

Queen Duck quacks at quiet quail,

Some quarters and a quilt.

Queen Duck's quack is really quite loud.

She can be heard above the crowd!

Queen Duck's quack is not quiet.

In fact, her quack is quite a riot!

The Race

Rooster and Rabbit raced in the rain,

Round the Red Road bend.

Running! Running!

From river to ranch,

To reach Raccoon at the end!

12

IF87101 "Fun"damental Phonics

Sipping Soup

Super Sarah sips her soup

With a super sort of spoon.

Its super size is so big,

Super Sarah's done too soon!

Silly Sally sips her soup

With a silly sort of spoon.

Its silly size is so, so small,

Silly Sally sips all afternoon!

Tiptoe Turtle

Tiny turtle,

Tiptoe to town,

Tiptoe up,

Tiptoe down.

Tiny turtle,

Tiptoe away,

Tiptoe tomorrow,

Tiptoe today.

IF87101 *"Fun"damental Phonics*

Visiting

In the valley,

On the vine,

Vegetables are very fine!

Visit the valley,

Visit the vine,

Visit the vegetables very fine!

✂ -

The Walk

Wait! Wait!

We're walking your way.

We'll wander the wide woods together.

Welcome along! We'll walk with a song

In this wonderful, warm walking weather.

14

IF87101 "Fun"damental Phonics

The One and Only You

You are you.

Yes, you are

Young and brave and free.

You are you

The whole year through—

Yet, you will never be me.

Each one of us is a one and only.

Being you is the best you can be!

Zooming Zebra

Zoom off to the zoo

To see a zebra with stripes

And other animals of all types.

Zoom off to the zoo

To see an ostrich's plume.

Zoom off to the zoo. Zoom, zoom, zoom!

IF87101 "Fun"damental Phonics

A Note to Teachers

At this point in your phonics work, you may be making the transition from beginning sounds to a study of ending consonants, along with long and short vowel sounds. A review can be helpful. One way to reinforce completed phonics work is to have your students make a booklet of the all the poems to this point. After students complete the books, suggest that they keep their booklets for reference as they progress to more difficult phonics concepts.

Note that /x/ is only presented as an ending consonant sound in this resource guide. In English, the true /x/ sound appears almost exclusively at the ends of words, and rarely as an onset sound.

Poems which present vowel sounds are marked in the answer key for the sound in any position within the word, but you may wish to have students work with them first as onset sounds only, depending on your methodology.

It's a Job

Want a job?
Scrub the tub.
Dust the cobwebs.
Plant the shrubs.
Grab an old bib,
Wipe out the crib.
Rub each knob—
That's your job!

IF87101 *"Fun"damental Phonics*

Dad Made Bread

Fred nodded his head
And hopped out of bed.
Mmm! Something smells so good!
Dad did what he said he would—
He baked fresh rolls and bread!

Jeff the Chef

Jeff, the chief chef,
Took a stiff lettuce leaf.
He cut off half
To stuff with beef.
But half a leaf
Was much too brief!

IF87101 "Fun"damental Phonics

Big Bag

In the big bag

Are a mug and a rag,

A wig and a flag,

A frog and a dog,

A twig and a log,

A bug and a jug,

A peg and a rug.

Oh no! This big bag

Is starting to sag!

The Yak

Look! Look! Look!

By the oak near the brook;

It's a yak with a book.

Look! Look! Look!

Quick, sneak a peek!

Will that yak read all week?

18

Seal in a Pool

Tell me, seal,

How do you feel?

In water so cool

I'd get a chill!

But you stay well

And never feel ill!

Sam the Clam

Sam the Clam swam

In the foam of the stream.

He swam to the dam,

Then awoke from his dream!

IF87101 "Fun"damental Phonics

Twin Queens

The queen has a grin
And a bright golden crown.
But the queen has a twin
Who wears only a frown.

Counting Sheep

To get to sleep,
I count sheep.
They step with pep,
Jump up and leap.
They skip and dip,
And hop and drop,
And flip and flop!
And when they stop,
I am fast asleep.

What to Wear?

Little bear sat in a chair.

Which sweater should he wear?

The one with a silly spider

Sipping from a glass of cider?

Or the one with purple flowers

Covered by soft rain showers?

This Class

Which class

Made this mess?

Broke this vase?

Made a fuss?

Lost the mouse?

Cracked this glass?

Missed the bus?

Guess.

Us?

Yes!

Not a Fit

This boot looks great,
But my foot is size eight.
That boot would fit fine
But it's a size nine!
Forget it . . . I'll have to wait!

Cave at the Cove

In the car we drove
To a seaside cove.
We decided to be brave
And explore a secret cave.
But we heard a roaring wave
And hurried from the cave!
Our quick move saved the day.

IF87101 "Fun"damental Phonics

Fix the Box

Ox and Fox
Sat on a box.
It broke as they tried to relax.
Fox said, "Ox,
Let's fix the box
With a mix of six tacks and wax!"

Buzz the Bumblebee

Buzz the Bumblebee goes buzz,

Out amid the pollen fuzz.

But when there is a breeze,

Buzz begins to sneeze.

Achoo! Achoo! Achoo!

At the hive, Buzz will laze,

Waiting for less windy days.

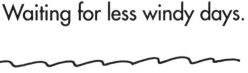

IF87101 "Fun"damental Phonics

Family Album

Annie! Come here!
Come! Come!
Look at this picture
In the family album.
Look, it's Annie
Eating apple pie.
Wish we had some!
Oh, my!

Exercise

The elves liked to do
Each exercise,
Much to the
Shoemaker's surprise!
So exhausted was
Elmer Elf
He couldn't even climb
Up to his shelf!

24

IF87101 "Fun"damental Phonics

In an Instant

In an instant,

An inchworm inches near.

In an instant,

It can disappear!

In an instant,

An insect digs a ditch.

In an instant,

You can scratch an itch!

Otter

Otter likes to play

With many things

Like olives, octagons,

And big, round rings.

Otter eats urchins,

Abalone and fish.

You won't see an

Omelet on his dish!

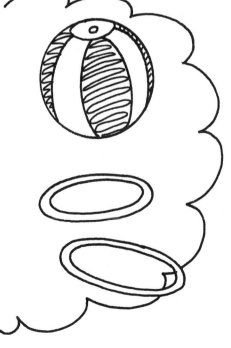

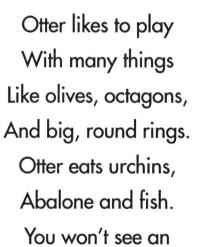

    IF87101 *"Fun"damental Phonics*

Umbrellas Up

An umbrella goes up.
An umbrella goes down.
People hide under umbrellas
All over town.
It's quite a funny sight,
To watch people frown,
When gusts of strong wind
Turn umbrellas upside-down.

Amy and Kate

On a day rainy and gray,
Amy and Kate stay inside to play.
They wear aprons to paint,
They shape some clay,
Until the rain goes away.
They are heard to say,
"May we go out today?"
"We may? Hooray!"

Easel Art

Paint a picture
On an easel
Of a single bee.
Or paint two or three
By a leafy tree.
But if a bee flies free
Near our arms or knees,
Let's flee!
Do you agree?

Sky Ideas

I can watch the sky
With the clouds passing by,
And spy the shapes that fly—
So can you, if you try!
I see islands and ice cream,
Brides, kites, and pipe dreams,
All of them light,
All of them white,
Fluffy, and bright.

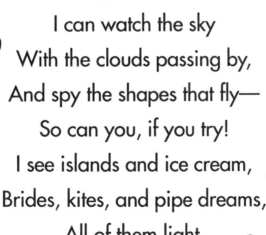

IF87101 *"Fun"damental Phonics*

Old Overalls

Oh! I like my overalls,
New or old, striped or bold.
Overalls are great to wear.
I own four pairs and I won't share!

1 2 3 4

Unique

Use a rocket
To fly up high
Through a bright and starry sky.
In all the universe,
You are unique,
Like each star and place
That astronauts seek.

IF87101 "Fun"damental Phonics

A B C Read the poem.

Circle each letter that makes the sound you hear at the beginning of  .

Bob's Bike

Bob bought a bike,
A beautiful bike,
With baskets on both sides.
They hold bats, boxes, and bags,
Now Bob has no room for rides!

Color the pictures that begin with the sound of the letter *b*.

Write.

B

b

IF87101 *"Fun"damental Phonics*

Read the poem.

Circle each letter that makes the sound you hear at the beginning of .

Come, Cozy Cat

Cute, cozy cat,
Curled up in a corner,
Care to come out for a break?

Circle the picture in each row that begins with the sound of the letter c.

Write.

© Instructional Fair • TS Denison

IF87101 "Fun"damental Phonics

Read the poem.

Circle each letter that makes the sound you hear at the beginning of .

Dinner Dishes

Dinner is done.
Dishes are dirty.
Doing each dish
Is a chore!

Circle each dish with a picture that starts with the sound of the letter *d*.

Write.

D _____

d _____

IF87101 *"Fun"damental Phonics*

A B C Read the poem.

Circle each letter that makes the sound you hear at the beginning of  .

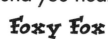

Foxy Fox

Foxy Fox found fifty figs
In a forest far away.
The figs were full,
The figs were fat.
The figs were falling.
Fancy that!

Color the pictures that begin with the sound of the letter *f*.

Write.

IF87101 "Fun"damental Phonics

Read the poem.

Circle each letter that makes the sound you hear at the beginning of .

Goat and Goose A-Gobbling

Down by the garden gate,
Goat and Goose
Gobbled their goods
Before it was too late!

Help Goat and Goose get out of the garden. Take the path with the pictures that begin with the sound of the letter *g*.

Write.

© Instructional Fair • TS Denison   IF87101 *"Fun"damental Phonics*

Name _____

Read the poem.

Circle each letter that makes the sound you hear at the beginning of  .

Helping Hands

Helping hands!
Hey! Hey, help!
Hurry to the hill!
Grab my hand
And help me stand.

Color the hand if the picture begins with the sound of the letter *h*.

Write.

IF87101 "Fun"damental Phonics

Read the poem.

Circle each letter that makes the sound you hear at the beginning of .

Jeep Ride

Jelly and jam
Bounce with a jolt and a jeer.
Jam on my jacket!
Jelly on my jeans!
It's sticky and I can't steer!

Color the jars with the pictures that begin with the sound of the letter *j.*

Write.

J

j

© Instructional Fair • TS Denison

IF87101 "Fun"damental Phonics

A B C Read the poem.

Circle each letter that makes the sound you hear at the beginning of .

Kangaroo Kick

Kangaroo, kick a kettle,
A kite or a key.
Kick any kind of thing,
Kangaroo.
Just don't kick me!

Circle all the pictures that begin with the sound of the letter *k*.

Write.

K _____

k _____

IF87101 "Fun"damental Phonics

Read the poem.

Circle each letter that makes the sound you hear at the beginning of 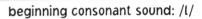 .

Library Lady

Library lady, look, look, look!
I'm looking for a library book.
Large or little, heavy or light,
I'm looking left and looking right!

Draw a line from the librarian to each book with a picture that starts with the sound of the letter *l*.

Write.

IF87101 "Fun"damental Phonics

ABC Read the poem.

Name _____

Circle each letter that makes the sound you hear at the beginning of .

Monday Morning March-Along

Monday morning,
Month of May,
Many mice march on their way
As Mister Mike milks the cow,
And Mister Cat moans, "Meow!"

If the picture begins with the sound of the letter *m*, color the space gray.

Write.

M

m

IF87101 "Fun"damental Phonics

Read the poem.

Circle each letter that makes the sound you hear at the beginning of .

Never a Noise

No nice neighbor next door.
Never a noise,
Nothing to notice,
Noon to night, what a bore!

Color the pictures in the night sky that begin with the sound of the letter *n*.

Write.

N __ __ __ __ __ __ __ __ __ __ __ __ __ __

n __ __ __ __ __ __ __ __ __ __ __ __ __ __

IF87101 *"Fun"damental Phonics*

A B C Read the poem.

Name _____

Circle each letter that makes the sound you hear at the beginning of  .

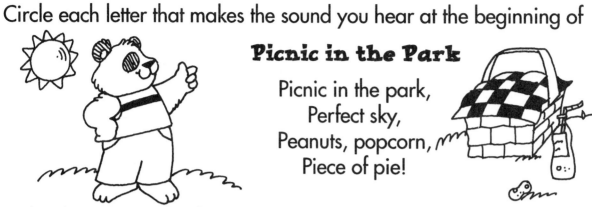

Picnic in the Park

Picnic in the park,
Perfect sky,
Peanuts, popcorn,
Piece of pie!

Color the pictures that begin with the sound of the letter *p* to help Panda find his way to the park.

Write.

P -

p -

40

Read the poem.

Circle each letter that makes the sound you hear at the beginning of .

Quacking Queen Duck

Queen Duck's quack is really quite loud
She can be heard above the crowd!
Queen Duck's quack is not quiet.
In fact, her quack is quite a riot!

Circle the picture in each row that begins with the sound of the letter q.

Write.

IF87101 "Fun"damental Phonics

A B C Read the poem.

Name _____

Circle each letter that makes the sound you hear at the beginning of .

The Race

Rooster and Rabbit raced in the rain,
Round the Red Road Bend.
Running! Running!
From river to ranch,
To reach Raccoon at the end!

Draw a line from Rabbit and Rooster to each picture that begins with the sound of the letter r.

Write.

R —

r —

42

A B C Read the poem.

Circle each letter that makes the sound you hear at the beginning of .

Sipping Soup

Super Sarah sips her soup
With a super sort of spoon.
Its super size is so big,
Super Sarah's done too soon!

Circle each picture in the kettle of soup that begins with the sound of the letter *s*.

Write.

S _ _ _ _ _ _ _ _ _ _ _ _ _ _ _ _ _ _

S _ _ _ _ _ _ _ _ _ _ _ _ _ _ _ _ _ _

IF87101 "Fun"damental Phonics

A B C Read the poem.

Name _____

Circle each letter that makes the sound you hear at the beginning of .

Tiptoe Turtle

Tiny turtle,
Tiptoe to town.
Tiptoe up,
Tiptoe down.

Help the turtle tiptoe to town. Take the path with the pictures that begin with the sound of the letter *t*.

Write.

_____

- - - - - - - - - - - - - - -

_____

_____

- - - - - - - - - - - - - - -

IF87101 *"Fun"damental Phonics*

A B C Read the poem.

Circle each letter that makes the sound you hear at the beginning of  .

Visiting

In the valley,
On the vine,
Vegetables are very fine!
Visit the valley, visit the vine,
Visit the vegetables very fine!

Color the vine leaves that have pictures that begin with the sound of the letter v.

Write.

V _ _ _ _ _ _ _ _ _ _ _ _ _ _ _ _

_ _ _ _ _ _ _ _ _ _ _ _ _ _ _ _ _

V _ _ _ _ _ _ _ _ _ _ _ _ _ _ _ _

IF87101 "Fun"damental Phonics

ABC Read the poem.

Circle each letter that makes the sound you hear at the beginning of 🕯️.

The Walk
Wait! Wait!
We're walking your way.
Welcome along!
We'll walk with a song.

Walk in the woods. Circle the pictures that begin with the sound of the letter *w*.

Write.

W

W

46

IF87101 "Fun"damental Phonics

A B C Read the poem.

Circle each letter that makes the sound you hear at the beginning of ⟨yo-yo⟩ .

The One and Only You

You are you
The whole year through—
Yet, you will never be me.
Each one of us is a one and only.
Being you is the best you can be!

Circle the picture in each row that begins with the sound of the letter y.

Write.

IF87101 "Fun"damental Phonics

A B C Read the poem.

Name _____

Circle each letter that makes the sound you hear at the beginning of .

Zooming Zebra

Zoom off to the zoo
To see a zebra with stripes
And other animals of all types.
Zoom off to the zoo. Zoom, zoom,
zoom!

Let's go to the zoo! Draw a line from the zebra to the pictures that begin with the sound of the letter z.

Write.

Z _

Z _

IF87101 "Fun"damental Phonics

Read the poem.

Circle each letter that makes the sound you hear at the end of .

It's a Job

Want a job?
Scrub the tub.
Rub each knob—
That's your job!

Say the name of each picture. If you hear the sound of the letter *b* at the end of the word, write the letter *b*. Leave the others blank.

cra	bi	ca
ba	pi	ja
we	ne	su

IF87101 *"Fun"damental Phonics*

Name _____

ending consonant sound: /d/

Read the poem.

Circle each letter that makes the sound you hear at the end of .

Dad Made Bread

Fred nodded his head
and hopped out of bed.
Dad did what he said he would—
He baked fresh rolls and bread!

Circle the picture in each row that ends with the sound of the letter *d*.

IF87101 "Fun"damental Phonics

Read the poem.

Circle each letter that makes the sound you hear at the end of .

Jeff the Chef

Jeff, the chief chef,
Took a stiff lettuce leaf.
He cut off half
To stuff with beef.

Color the pictures that end with the sound of the letter *f*.

IF87101 "Fun"damental Phonics

Read the poem.

Circle each letter that makes the sound you hear at the end of .

Big Bag

In the big bag
Are a mug and a rag,
A wig and a flag,
A frog and a dog,
A twig and a log...
This big bag is starting to sag!

Write the letter g on the line if the picture ends with the sound of the letter g.

IF87101 *"Fun"damental Phonics*

Read the poem.

Circle each letter that makes the sound you hear at the end of  .

The Yak

Look! Look! Look!
By the oak near the brook;
It's a yak with a book!
Look! Look! Look!
Quick, sneak a peek!
Will that yak read all week?

Write the letter *k* on the line if the picture ends with the sound of the letter *k*.

IF87101 "Fun"damental Phonics

Read the poem.

Circle each letter that makes the sound you hear at the end of .

Seal in a Pool

Tell me, seal:
How do you feel?
In water this cool,
I'd get a chill!
But you stay well
And never feel ill!

Draw a circle around the pictures that end with the sound of the letter *l*. Then write the letter *l* on those lines.

IF87101 *"Fun"damental Phonics*

A B C Read the poem.

Circle each letter that makes the sound you hear at the end of 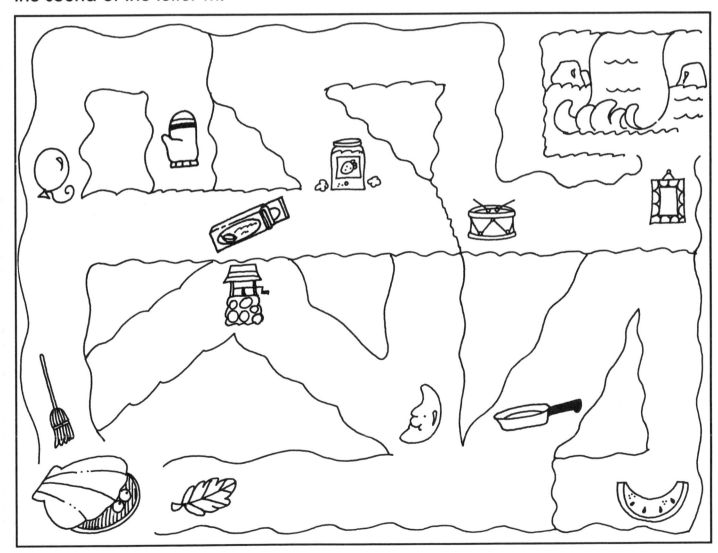 .

Sam the Clam

Sam the Clam swam
In the foam in the stream.
He swam to the dam
Then awoke from his dream!

Help Sam find his way to the dam. Take the path with the pictures that end with the sound of the letter *m*.

IF87101 "Fun"damental Phonics

ABC

Read the poem.

Circle each letter that makes the sound you hear at the end of .

Twin Queens

The queen has a grin
And a bright golden crown.
But the queen has a twin
Who wears only a frown.

Color the jewels on the crown if the picture ends with the sound of the letter *n*.

Read the poem.

Circle each letter that makes the sound you hear at the end of  .

Counting Sheep

To get to sleep
I count sheep.
They step with pep,
Jump up and leap!
And when they stop,
I am fast asleep.

Color the sheep with pictures that end with the sound of the letter *p*. Then write the letter *p* on those lines.

57

Read the poem.

Circle each letter that makes the sound you hear at the end of 🐻 .

What to Wear?

Little bear sat in a chair.
Which sweater should he wear?
The one with the silly spider
Sipping from a glass of cider?
Or the one with purple flowers
Covered by soft rain showers?

Draw a line from the bear to each sweater that has a picture that ends with the sound of the letter *r*.

IF87101 "Fun"damental Phonics

Name _____

Read the poem.

Circle each letter that makes the sound you hear at the end of  .

This Class

Which class
Made this mess?
Made a fuss?
Missed the bus?
Guess.
Us?
Yes!

Color each picture that ends with the sound of the letter *s*. Then write the letter *s* on those lines.

59

IF87101 *"Fun"damental Phonics*

Name _____

Read the poem.

Circle each letter that makes the sound you hear at the end of .

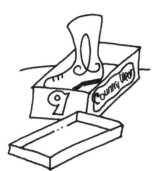

Not a Fit

This boot looks great,
But my foot is size eight.
That boot would fit fine
But it's a size nine!

Write *t* on the lines on each boot. Then match each "t" boot to a boot whose picture ends with the sound of the letter *t*.

IF87101 "Fun"damental Phonics

Read the poem.

Circle each letter that makes the sound you hear at the end of .

Cave at the Cove

In the car we drove
To a seaside cove.
We decided to be brave
And explore a secret cave.

Color the pictures that end with the sound of v.

Read the poem.

Circle each letter that makes the sound you hear at the end of ⬚ .

Fix the Box

Ox and Fox
Sat on a box.
It broke as they tried to relax.
Fox said, "Ox,
Let's fix the box
With a mix of six tacks and
wax!"

Look in the box. Color the pictures that end with the sound of the letter x. Then write x on those lines.

IF87101 "Fun"damental Phonics

Read the poem.

Circle each letter that makes the sound you hear at the end of .

Buzz the Bumblebee

Buzz the Bumblebee goes buzz,
Out amid the pollen fuzz.
But when there is a breeze,
Buzz begins to sneeze.
Achoo! Achoo! Achoo!

Help Buzz get back home. Take the path with pictures that end with the sound of the letter z.

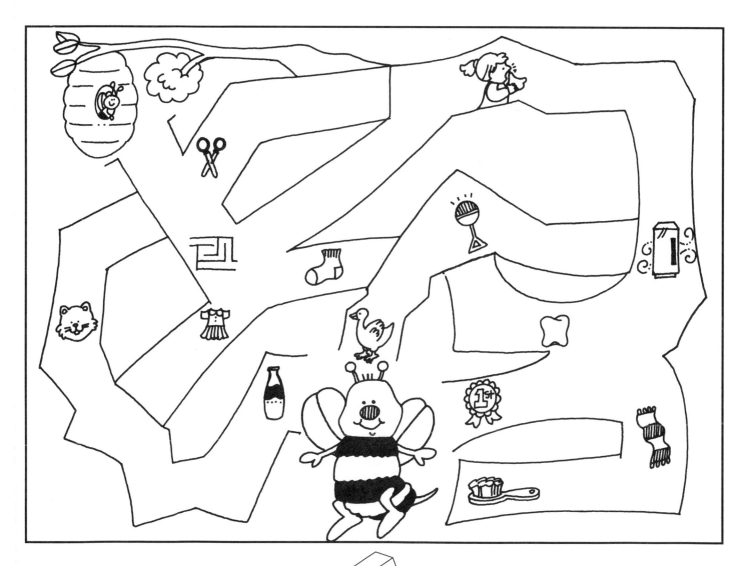

IF87101 "Fun"damental Phonics

Read the poem.

Circle each letter *a* that is making a short *a* sound.

Family Album

Annie! Come here!
Come! Come!
Look at this picture in the family album.
Look, it's Annie
Eating apple pie.

Color the pictures that begin with the sound of short *a*.

Write.

IF87101 "Fun"damental Phonics

Read the poem.

Circle each letter e that is making a short e sound.

Exercise

The elves liked to do
Each exercise...
So exhausted was Elmer Elf
He couldn't even climb
Up to his shelf!

Draw a line from the elf to each picture that begins with the short e sound.

Write.

E e

IF87101 "Fun"damental Phonics

Read the poem.

Circle each letter *i* that is making a short *i* sound.

In an Instant

In an instant,
An inchworm inches near.
In an instant,
It can disappear!

Color each picture on the inchworm that begins with the short *i* sound.

IF87101 *"Fun"damental Phonics*

Ending Consonant Sound Cards: crab, bib, web, bread, bed, cloud, leaf, scarf, wolf, tag, pig, egg, hook, book, brick, shell, wheel, ball, drum, broom

© Instructional Fair • TS Denison

IF87101 "Fun"damental Phonics

Ending Consonant Sound Cards: jam, pin, chain, acorn, cup, soap, harp, flower, four, star, bus, nurse, bat, hat, hive, five, ax, box, maze, prize

IF87101 "Fun"damental Phonics

Read the poem.

Circle each letter o that is making a short o sound.

Otter

Otter likes to play
With many things
Like olives, octagons,
And big, round rings.

Otter only thinks about things that begin with the short o sound. Circle each picture that starts with the sound of short o.

October

Write.

_____

IF87101 *"Fun"damental Phonics*

Read the poem.

Circle each letter *u* that is making a short *u* sound.

Umbrellas Up

An umbrella goes up,
An umbrella goes down.
People hide under umbrellas
All over town.

Write *U u* on the lines on each umbrella. Then draw a line from each umbrella to a picture that starts with the short *u* sound.

IF87101 "Fun"damental Phonics

Read the poem.

Circle each letter *a* that is making a long *a* sound.

Amy and Kate

On a day rainy and gray,
Amy and Kate stay inside to play.
They wear aprons to paint,
They shape some clay,
Until the rain goes away.

Here are pictures that Amy and Kate painted! Color the pictures that start with the sound of long *a*.

April

Write.

Aa

© Instructional Fair • TS Denison

IF87101 "Fun"damental Phonics

Read the poem. Name _____

Circle each letter e that is making a long e sound.

Easel Art
Paint a picture
On an easel
Of a single bee.
Or paint two or three
By a leafy tree.

Use a green crayon to draw a circle around the pictures that start with the long e sound.

Write.

E e

70

Name _____

Read the poem.

Circle each letter *i* that is making a long *i* sound.

Sky Ideas

I see islands and ice cream,
Brides, kites and pipe dreams,
All of them white,
Fluffy and bright.

Write *i* on each cloud. Then draw a line from each cloud to a picture that starts with the long *i* sound.

71

IF87101 "Fun"damental Phonics

Read the poem.

Circle each letter *o* that is making a long *o* sound.

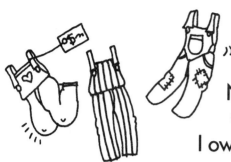

Old Overalls

Oh! I like my overalls,
New or old, striped or bold.
Overalls are great to wear.
I own four pairs and I won't share!

Use an orange crayon to color the patches that have pictures that begin with the long *o* sound.

Write.

IF87101 *"Fun"damental Phonics*

Read the poem.

Circle each letter *u* that is making a long *u* sound.

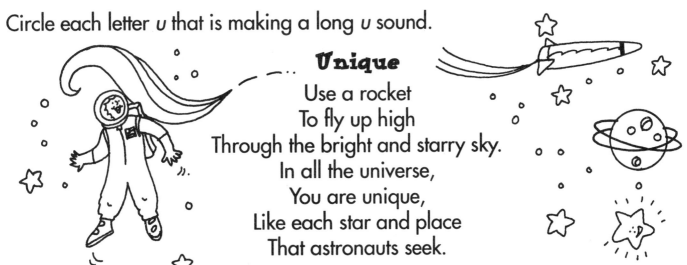

Unique

Use a rocket
To fly up high
Through the bright and starry sky.
In all the universe,
You are unique,
Like each star and place
That astronauts seek.

Draw a line from the unicorn to the pictures that start with the long *u* sound.

Write.

U u

IF87101 "Fun"damental Phonics

ABC Read the poem.

Circle the two letters that make the sound you hear at the beginning of .

Blizzard

Blizzard blowing
On our block!
Blow! Blow!
Blasts of snow!

Find your way through the blowing blizzard. Take the path with the pictures that begin with the sound of *bl.*

Write.

 _

Read the poem.

Circle the two letters that make the sound you hear at the beginning of .

Brown Bread

Brown bread
For breakfast
Brought to my room!
Breakfast crumbs need brushing up—
Bring me the broom!

Color the pictures that begin with the sound of *br*.

Write.

_____

_____

IF87101 "Fun"damental Phonics

Name _____

Read the poem.

Circle the two letters that make the sound you hear at the beginning of .

Clean the Clouds
Climb up
And clean these clouds!
We can't see up here.
Take a cloth
And clean up close
Until each cloud is clear!

Color each cloud with a picture that begins with the sound of *cl*.

Write.

C l _ _ _ _ _ _ _ _ _ _

IF87101 *"Fun"damental Phonics*

Name _____

Read the poem.

Circle the two letters that make the sound you hear at the beginning of .

Crackers and Cream

Crackers and cream
With cranberry crumble.
What a crazy lunch!
But I won't grumble,
Cry or mumble,
Instead, I'll crunch, crunch, crunch!

Draw a line from the pitcher of cream to each cracker with a picture that begins with the sound of *cr*.

Write.

_____

IF87101 *"Fun"damental Phonics*

Read the poem.

Circle the two letters that make the sound you hear at the beginning of .

Dragon Dream

A dragon is drinking
From the dripping drain.
Now it's dragging
My dresser drawer!
It's drumming my drum,
It's drying a dress—
Oh, dear! I'm dreaming some more!

Circle the pictures that begin with the sound of *dr*.

Write.

d r --

IF87101 "Fun"damental Phonics

Read the poem.

Circle the two letters that make the sound you hear at the beginning of .

Flying Fly
The fly flew to the flower.
The fly flew to the floor.
The fly flipped,
The fly flopped,
The fly flew out the door!

Help the fly find the door. Take the path with the pictures that begin with the sound of *fl*.

Write.

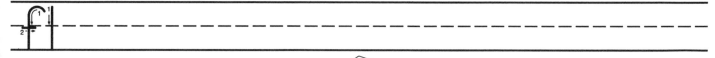

IF87101 *"Fun"damental Phonics*

Read the poem.

Circle the two letters that make the sound you hear at the beginning of  .

My Friend Fred

My friend Fred
Eats fresh fruit
And French fries,
While Fred's frog
Eats fresh flies!

Color each space green if the picture begins with the sound of *fr*. Color the other spaces blue.

Write.

 _____

_____ 80 _____

Read the poem.

Circle the two letters that make the sound you hear at the beginning of .

Great Grapes

Grab a bunch of green grapes,
The greatest snack around!
But *never* grab the green grass
Growing in the ground!

Color the grapes that have pictures that begin with the sound of *gr*.

Write.

gr

     IF87101 *"Fun"damental Phonics*

Read the poem.

Circle the two letters that make the sound you hear at the beginning of .

Pretending

Let's pretend
We're prince and princess,
Very proud and pretty.
People will praise us,
Present us with prizes
As we protect our city!

Write *pr* on the lines below the pictures that begin with the sound of *pr*.

Write.

_____

pr _____

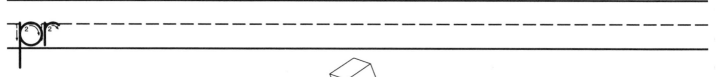

consonant blends: /sc/

Read the poem.

Circle the two letters that make the sound you hear at the beginning of  .

Scoot
The scarecrow
Has a scary scarf
To scare the crows away.
Scoot! Scat!
Scatter, crows!
Scoot and stay away!

Draw a line from the scarecrow to the pictures that begin with the sound of *sc*.

Write.

SC

IF87101 "Fun"damental Phonics

A B C Read the poem.

Circle the two letters that make the sound you hear at the beginning of .

Sledding

Never sleep on a sled!
Never sleep on a sled!
You'll slip and slide,
It's a slippery ride,
No, never sleep on a sled!

Write the letters *sl* on the lines next to the pictures that begin with the sound of *sl*.

Write.

S l _____

IF87101 *"Fun"damental Phonics*

A B C Read the poem.

Circle the two letters that make the sound you hear at the beginning of .

Snake and Snail

Snake and Snail
Sniffed in the snow,
Which muffled their snuffle attack.
Snake sneezed!
Snail sneezed!
Snow was on their backs!

Color the picture in each box that begins with the sound of *sn*.

Write.

sn

IF87101 *"Fun"damental Phonics*

Name _____

Read the poem.

Circle the two letters that make the sound you hear at the beginning of .

Spaghetti

Without a single spatter,
I can spin spaghetti on my spoon.
Oops! A big spaghetti spill!
I guess I spoke too soon!

Write the letters *sp* below each spoon that has a picture that begins with the sound of *sp*.

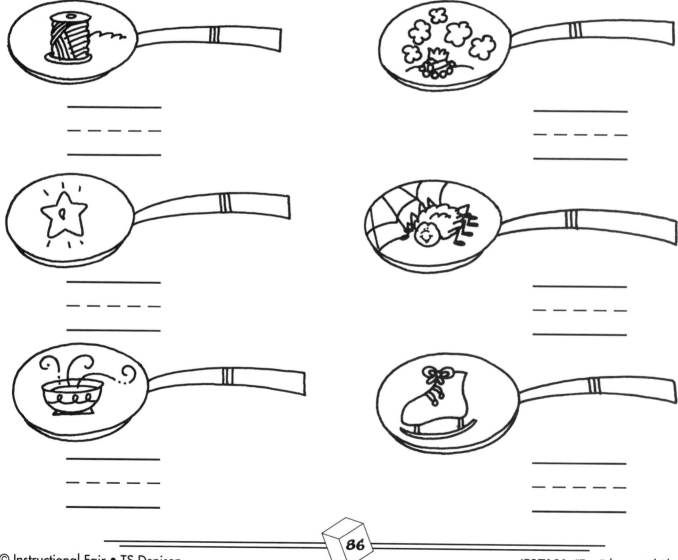

_____ _____

_____ _____

_____ _____

IF87101 "Fun"damental Phonics

Name _____

Read the poem.

Circle the two letters that make the sound you hear at the beginning of   .

Stop!

Stop! Don't step up!
Stay put! Stand still!
Sticks and stones
Are on those stairs.
You may start to
Stumble there!

Color each stone that has a picture that begins with the sound of *st*.

Write.

S̶t̶

IF87101 *"Fun"damental Phonics*

Read the poem.

Circle the two letters that make the sound you hear at the beginning of  .

Swimming Swan

A swimming swan
Is swift and sweet,
So sweet it sweeps me
Off my feet!

Draw a line from the swan to each word that begins with the sound of *sw*.

Write.

_____

S W _

_____

IF87101 *"Fun"damental Phonics*

A B C

Read the poem.

Name _____

Circle the two letters that make the sound you hear at the beginning of  .

Travel by Train

Travel by train!
The trip is a treat.
When trucks and trailers
Are trapped in traffic,
Train tracks can't be beat.

Take a train ride! Color the pictures that begin with the sound of *tr*.

Write.

IF87101 *"Fun"damental Phonics*

Read the poem.

Circle the words that end in *ap*.

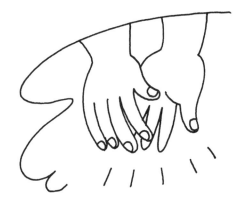

Clap and Tap

Hands clap!
Arms flap!
Fingers snap!
Feet tap!
Knuckles rap!

Read each sentence and look at the picture clue. Write the *ap* word on each line. Then write that word in its numbered space in the puzzle.

1. I had a _____ .

2. Look at the _____ .

3. The baby took a _____ .

4. Look at the mouse _____ .

5. My fingers _____ .

6. I can _____ .

IF87101 "Fun"damental Phonics

Read the poem.

Circle the words ending in *ell*.

Nell's Bell

Nell has a bell
She wants to sell.
It's shaped like a shell
And rings very well.
Its sound is swell!
Listen! Can you tell?

Look at the picture and write the *ell* word on the line. Then find each word in the bell puzzle and circle it.

1. _____

2. _____

3. _____

4. _____

5. _____

6. _____

```
s  b  e  l  l
n  y  e  l  l
p  s  e  l  l  d  w
s  m  e  l  l  t  e
f  e  d  g  p  l  l
s  h  e  l  l  l  l
```

IF87101 "Fun"damental Phonics

A B C Read the poem.

Circle the words ending in *ill*.

Such a Thrill

It's such a thrill
To have the skill
To climb a hill
Without a spill!

Write *ill* on each line. Then circle the correct picture for each word you write.

IF87101 *"Fun"damental Phonics*

Read the poem.

Name _____

Circle the words ending in *ot*.

Hot Pot!

See that pot?
That pot is hot!
How hot it got!
It's hot *a lot*!

Write the word for each picture on the line. Use the Word Bank to help you.

1.  _____

4.  _____

2. _____

5. _____

3. _____

6. _____

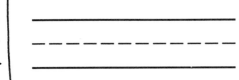

Word Bank

dot	spot	trot
cot	pot	hot

IF87101 *"Fun"damental Phonics*

Read the poem.

Circle the words ending in *ug*.

A Bug
Did you see the bug
Under the rug?
Quick! Get a jug!
We will bug that bug,
So he's not so smug
Under his snug rug.

Write the word on the lines next to the picture. Then connect the dots in the same order as your answers.

1. _____

2. _____

3. _____

4. _____

5. _____

6. _____

It is a _____ .

IF87101 "Fun"damental Phonics

Read the poem.

Circle the words ending in *ake*.

Don't Shake a Snake!

Never use a rake
To give a snake a shake
Just to see if it's awake!
For goodness sake!

Write the word on the lines under each
picture. Use the Word Bank to help you.
Then find and circle the words in the puzzle.

Word Bank

snake	lake	flake
cake	rake	bake

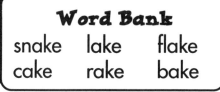

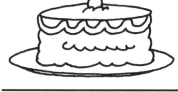

_____

_____

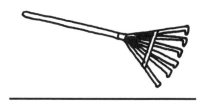

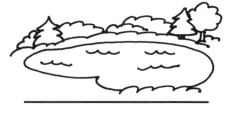

_____

_____

a	b	a	k	e	s	r	a	k	e	r
s	n	a	k	e	c	a	k	e	k	e
k	l	a	k	e	e	f	l	a	k	e

IF87101 "Fun"damental Phonics

Read the poem.

Circle the words ending in *eat*.

Wheat

What is wheat?
It is grain, not meat.
Tall and gold in the summer heat,
Cutting it is quite a feat!
Then it's baked into the bread we eat.

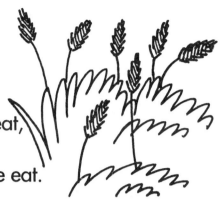

Write the word on the lines under each
picture. Use the Word Bank to help you.
Find and circle the words in the puzzle.

Word Bank

seat	beat	meat
pleat	heat	eat

_____

- - - - - - - - - - -

_____

_____

- - - - - - - - - - -

_____

j	d	b	e	a	t	v	c	p	a	b	l	n
e	m	b	r	y	e	a	g	y	h	e	a	t
a	s	d	a	p	l	e	a	t	l	g	e	o
t	z	m	e	a	t	e	m	c	a	e	w	f
b	f	e	h	k	t	b	t	s	e	a	t	s

96

IF87101 *"Fun"damental Phonics*

Read the poem.

long-vowel word families: /ide/

Circle the words ending in *ide*.

Slide Ride

Let's both glide
Down the slide outside.
It's tall and wide,
For a fast, wild ride!

Write the word below each picture. Use the Word Bank to help you. Then find and circle the words in the puzzle.

Word Bank

slide   side   ride
bride   hide   inside

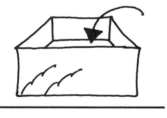

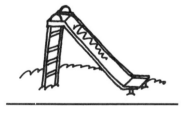

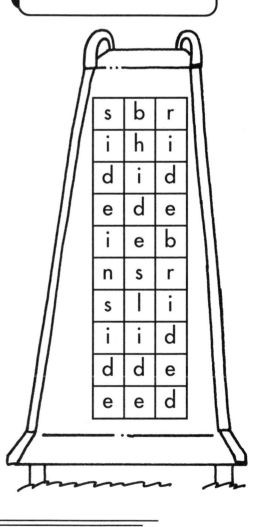

s	b	r
i	h	i
d	i	d
e	d	e
i	e	b
n	s	r
s	l	i
i	i	d
d	d	e
e	e	d

© Instructional Fair • TS Denison

IF87101 "Fun"damental Phonics

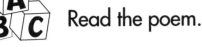

Read the poem.

Name _____

Circle the words ending in *oat*.

Silly Goat
A silly goat
Jumped off a boat
To swim and float.
He had no coat!
Though he loved to float,
He got a sore throat!

Write the word for each picture on the
lines. Use the Word Bank to help you.
Then write the words in the puzzle.

Word Bank

goat	boat	float
coat	moat	oat

Across

_____

3. _____

_____

4. _____

_____

6. _____

Down

_____

1. _____

_____

2. _____

_____

5. _____

98

Blast Off!

A multi-skill game for large or small groups.

**reparation**

Create a small pocket folder for each student. Have students illustrate the front cover. You can use the template of a rocket blasting off from a launch pad (page 100), or have your students create their own designs.

Fold bottom of paper or tagboard up 2 inches.
Staple along the edges.

Fold in half.

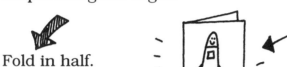

Provide each student with a set of letter cards (pages 101-104). Choose sounds on which you wish to focus, and have students remove those cards from their packs. Ask them to place the cards on the tabletop or floor in front of them.

nstructions:

Explain that you will say a word and they are to listen for the beginning blend. When they find the card that makes that sound, they should put it in the pocket, and close the folder. When all the folders are closed, call "Blast Off!" Students open their folders and hold them up so you can see which card they chose.

Note: You may find it helpful to demonstrate this using an enlarged folder and letter cards if you are instructing the whole group. After demonstrating, have the students try the activity, helping one another before they work alone.

ariations:

- Spell simple words using consonant blend and phonograms (word families). **Example:** Say /fr/. Have students repeat the sound. Then have them choose the card for that blend. Then say the phonogram *ame*. Repeat the complete word blending the two parts. Students should choose the correct word family card and place both cards in the correct order to spell the word.

- Give the ending letters for a phonogram/word family. Students should place the letters in their folders and choose a blend to create a new word. After placing the blend in front of the word ending they should close the folder. Call on students to say the sounds of the letters they selected and then the whole word they have created.

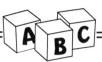

Cover design for Blast Off!

Duplicate this cover design. Have
your students cut out and color the
rocket graphic. Then instruct them
to paste the rocket in the center of
their Blast Off! folder covers.

bl	br	cl	cr	dr
fl	fr	gr	pr	sc
sl	sn	sp	st	sw

101

IF87101 *"Fun"damental Phonics*

tr	ap	at	ed	ell
en	et	ig	ill	in
it	ob	og	op	ot

IF87101 *"Fun"damental Phonics*

ub	ug	um	ut	ake
ame	ape	ate	ail	ain
eed	eel	eep	eam	eat

IF87101 *"Fun"damental Phonics*

eet	ide	ine	ive	ole
one	oad	oal		
oat				

IF87101 *"Fun"damental Phonics*

Beginning Consonant Sound Cards: butterfly, balloon, camel, cap, dinosaur, dog, fish, fork, goose, glove, hippo, hammer, jacket, jet, kite, key, lemon, lollipop, magnet, mushroom

IF87101 "Fun"damental Phonics

Beginning Consonant Sound Cards: newspaper, net, pirate, puppet, quail, quilt, rattle, rainbow, sock, scissors, tooth, table, van, valentine, wagon, watermelon, yarn, yak, zipper, zebra

IF87101 "Fun"damental Phonics

Beginning Consonant Blend Sound Cards: block, bridge, clown, crown, dragon, dress, fly, flag, frog, grapes, princess, scale, scarecrow, sled, snake, snail, spoon, stool, swan, train

IF87101 "Fun"damental Phonics

Short- and Long-Vowel Phonogram Cards: cap, map, bell, well, grill, hill, cot, pot, plug, rug, cake, lake, rake, wheat, feet, slide, bride, coat, goat, boat

Answer Key

"Fun"damental Phonics
1st Grade

Page 29

Page 30

IF87101 "Fun"damental Phonics

Page 31

Read the poem.

Circle each letter that makes the sound you hear at the beginning of 🍽️.

Dinner Dishes

Dinner is done.
Dishes are dirty.
Doing each dish
Is a chore!

Circle each dish with a picture that starts with the sound of the letter d.

Write.

D

d

© Instructional Fair • TS Denison   IF87101 "Fun"damental Phonics

Page 31

Page 32

Read the poem.

Circle each letter that makes the sound you hear at the beginning of 🦊.

Foxy Fox

Foxy Fox found fifty figs
In a forest far away.
The figs were full,
The figs were fat.
The figs were falling.
Fancy that!

Color the pictures that begin with the sound of the letter f.

Write.

F

f

© Instructional Fair • TS Denison   IF87101 "Fun"damental Phonics

Page 32

Page 33

Read the poem.

Circle each letter that makes the sound you hear at the beginning of 🐐.

Goat and Goose A-Gobbling

Down by the garden gate,
Goat and Goose
Gobbled their goods
Before it was too late!

Help Goat and Goose get out of the garden. Take the path with the pictures that begin with the sound of the letter g.

Write.

G

g

© Instructional Fair • TS Denison   IF87101 "Fun"damental Phonics

Page 33

Page 34

Read the poem.

Circle each letter that makes the sound you hear at the beginning of 🔨.

Helping Hands

Helping hands!
Hey! Hey, help!
Hurry to the hill!
Grab my hand
And help me stand.

Color the hand if the picture begins with the sound of the letter h.

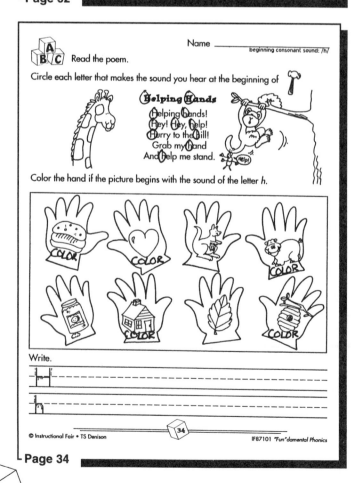

Write.

H

h

© Instructional Fair • TS Denison   IF87101 "Fun"damental Phonics

Page 34

© Instructional Fair • TS Denison   IF87101 "Fun"damental Phonics

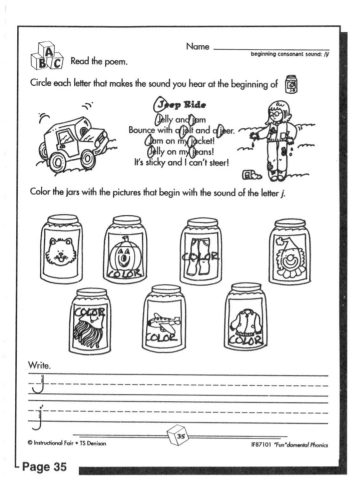

Page 35

beginning consonant sound: /j/

Read the poem.

Circle each letter that makes the sound you hear at the beginning of

Jeep Ride

Jelly and jam
Bounce with a jolt and a jeer.
Jam on my jacket!
Jelly on my jeans!
It's sticky and I can't steer!

Color the jars with the pictures that begin with the sound of the letter j.

Write.

J

j

© Instructional Fair • TS Denison

35

IF87101 "Fun"damental Phonics

Page 36

beginning consonant sound: /k/

Read the poem.

Circle each letter that makes the sound you hear at the beginning of

Kangaroo Kick

Kangaroo kick a kettle,
A kite or a key.
Kick any kind of thing,
Kangaroo.
Just don't kick me!

Circle all the pictures that begin with the sound of the letter k.

Write.

K

k

© Instructional Fair • TS Denison

36

IF87101 "Fun"damental Phonics

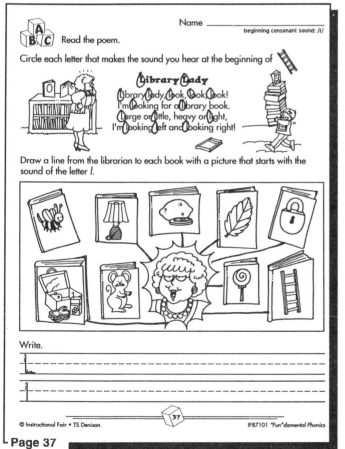

Page 37

beginning consonant sound: /l/

Read the poem.

Circle each letter that makes the sound you hear at the beginning of

Library Lady

Library lady, look, look, look!
I'm looking for a library book.
Large or little, heavy or light,
I'm looking left and looking right!

Draw a line from the librarian to each book with a picture that starts with the sound of the letter l.

Write.

l

l

© Instructional Fair • TS Denison

37

IF87101 "Fun"damental Phonics

Page 38

beginning consonant sound: /m/

Read the poem.

Circle each letter that makes the sound you hear at the beginning of

Monday Morning March-Along

Monday morning,
Month of May,
Many mice march on their way
As Mister Mike milks the cow,
And Mister Cat moans, "Meow!"

If the picture begins with the sound of the letter m, color the space gray.

Write.

M

m

© Instructional Fair • TS Denison

38

IF87101 "Fun"damental Phonics

© Instructional Fair • TS Denison

IF87101 "Fun"damental Phonics

Name _____

beginning consonant sound: /n/

ABC Read the poem.

Circle each letter that makes the sound you hear at the beginning of 🌙 .

Never a Noise

Notice neighbor next door.
Never a noise,
Nothing to notice,
Noon to night, what a bore!

Color the pictures in the night sky that begin with the sound of the letter *n*.

Write.

N

n

Name _____

beginning consonant sound: /p/

ABC Read the poem.

Circle each letter that makes the sound you hear at the beginning of 🐼 .

Picnic in the Park

Picnic in the park,
Perfect sky,
Peanuts, popcorn,
Piece of pie!

Color the pictures that begin with the sound of the letter *p* to help Panda find his way to the park.

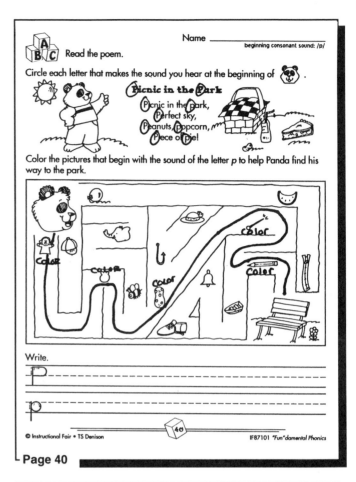

Write.

P

p

Name _____

beginning consonant sound: /q/

ABC Read the poem.

Circle each letter that makes the sound you hear at the beginning of 👑 .

Quacking Queen Duck

Queen Duck's quack is really quite loud
She can be heard above the crowd!
Queen Duck's quack is not quiet.
In fact, her quack is quite a riot!

Circle the picture in each row that begins with the sound of the letter *q*.

Write.

Q

q

Name _____

beginning consonant sound: /r/

ABC Read the poem.

Circle each letter that makes the sound you hear at the beginning of 🐰 .

The Race

Rooster and Rabbit raced in the rain,
Round the Red Road Bend.
Running! Running!
From river to ranch,
To reach Raccoon at the end!

Draw a line from Rabbit and Rooster to each picture that begins with the sound of the letter *r*.

Write.

R

r

ABC Read the poem.

Circle each letter that makes the sound you hear at the beginning of 🥄

Sipping Soup

Super Sarah sips her soup
With a super sort of spoon.
Its super size is so big,
Super Sarah's done too soon!

Circle each picture in the kettle of soup that begins with the sound of the letter *s*.

Write.

S

S

IF87101 *"Fun"damental Phonics*

ABC Read the poem.

Circle each letter that makes the sound you hear at the beginning of

Tiptoe Turtle

Tiny turtle,
Tiptoe to town.
Tiptoe up,
Tiptoe down.

Help the turtle tiptoe to town. Take the path with the pictures that begin with the sound of the letter *t*.

Write.

T

t

IF87101 *"Fun"damental Phonics*

ABC Read the poem.

Circle each letter that makes the sound you hear at the beginning of

Visiting

In the valley,
On the vine,
Vegetables are very fine!
Visit the valley, visit the vine,
Visit the vegetables very fine!

Color the vine leaves that have pictures that begin with the sound of the letter *v*.

COLOR

COLOR

COLOR

COLOR Mine

Write.

V

V

IF87101 *"Fun"damental Phonics*

ABC Read the poem.

Circle each letter that makes the sound you hear at the beginning of

The Walk

Wait! Wait!
We're walking your way.
Welcome along!
We'll walk with a song.

Walk in the woods. Circle the pictures that begin with the sound of the letter *w*.

Write.

W

W

IF87101 *"Fun"damental Phonics*

IF87101 *"Fun"damental Phonics*

Page 47

beginning consonant sound: /y/

A B C Read the poem.

Circle each letter that makes the sound you hear at the beginning of 🔴

The One and Only You

You are you
The whole year through—
Yet, you will never be me.
Each one of us is a one and only.
Being you is the best you can be!

Circle the picture in each row that begins with the sound of the letter y.

Write.

Y

y

Page 48

beginning consonant sound: /z/

A B C Read the poem.

Circle each letter that makes the sound you hear at the beginning of 🦔

Zooming Zebra

Zoom off to the zoo
To see a zebra with stripes
And other animals of all types.
Zoom off to the zoo. Zoom, zoom,
zoom!

Let's go to the zoo! Draw a line from the zebra to the pictures that begin with the sound of the letter z.

Write.

Z

z

Page 49

ending consonant sound: /b/

A B C Read the poem.

Circle each letter that makes the sound you hear at the end of 🛁

It's a Job

Want a job?
Scrub the tub.
Rub each knob.
That's your job!

Say the name of each picture. If you hear the sound of the letter b at the end of the word, write the letter b. Leave the others blank.

crab	bib	ca
ba	pi	ja
web	ne	sub

Page 50

ending consonant sound: /d/

A B C Read the poem.

Circle each letter that makes the sound you hear at the end of 🍞.

Dad Made Bread

Fred nodded his head
and hopped out of bed.
Dad did what he said he would.
He baked fresh rolls and bread!

Circle the picture in each row that ends with the sound of the letter d.

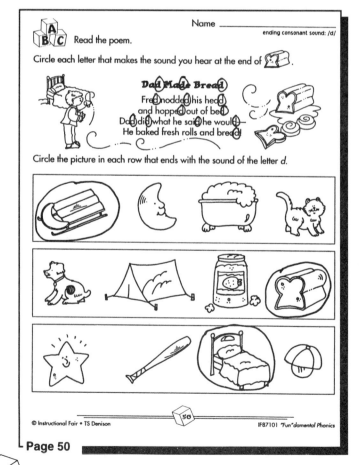

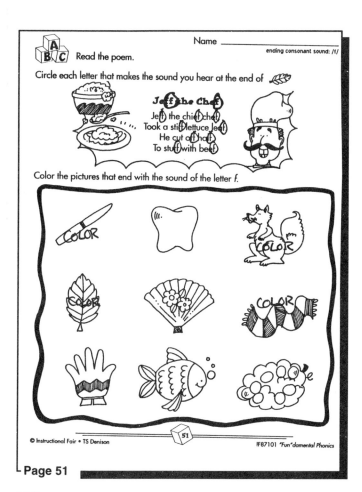

Page 51

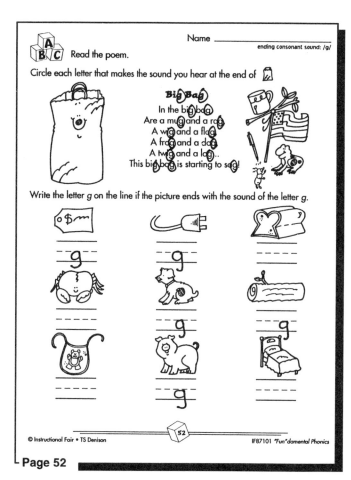

Page 52

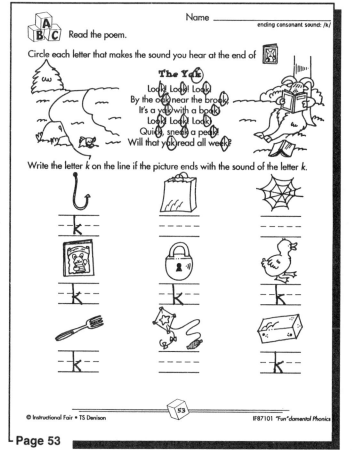

Page 53

Page 54

IF87101 *"Fun"damental Phonics*

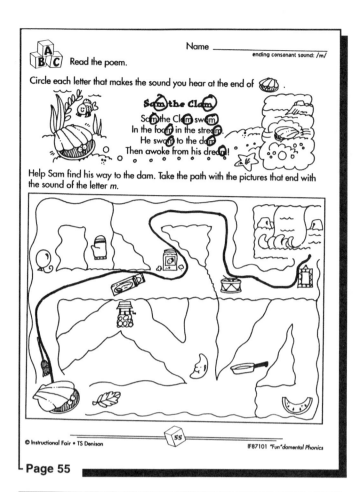

Page 55

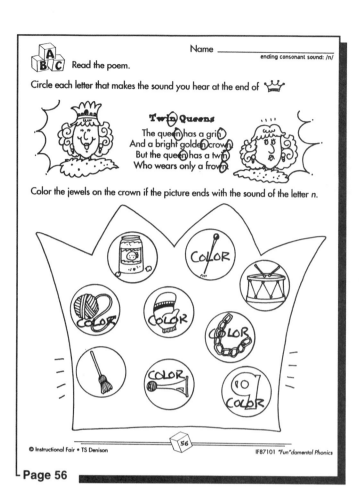

Page 56

Page 57

Page 58

Page 59

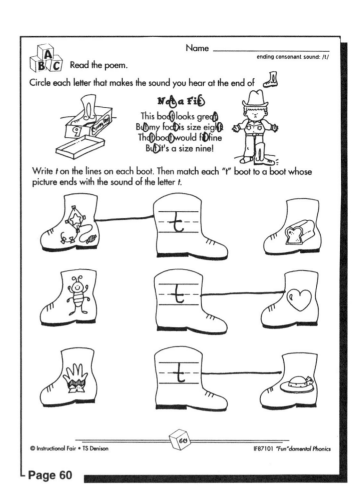

Page 60

Page 61

Page 62

Page 63

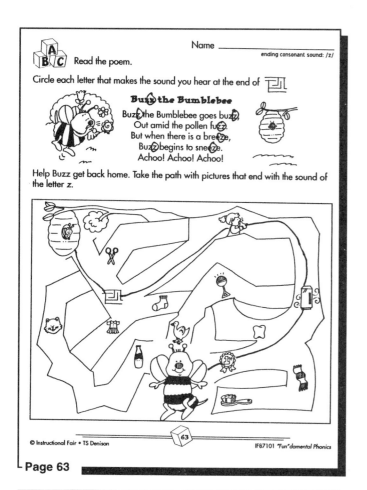

A B C Read the poem.

Name _____

Circle each letter that makes the sound you hear at the end of 🔒

Buzz the Bumblebee

Buzz the Bumblebee goes buzz,
Out amid the pollen fuzz.
But when there is a breeze,
Buzz begins to sneeze.
Achoo! Achoo! Achoo!

Help Buzz get back home. Take the path with pictures that end with the sound of the letter z.

© Instructional Fair • TS Denison   63   IF87101 "Fun"damental Phonics

Page 64

A B C Read the poem.

Name _____

Circle each letter a that is making a short a sound.

Family Album

Annie! Come here!
Come! Come!
Look at this picture in the family album.
Look, it's Annie
Eating apple pie.

Color the pictures that begin with the sound of short a.

Write.

A a _ _ _ _ _ _ _ _ _ _

© Instructional Fair • TS Denison   64   IF87101 "Fun"damental Phonics

Page 65

A B C Read the poem.

Name _____

Circle each letter e that is making a short e sound.

Exercise

The elves liked to do
Each exercise...
So exhausted was Elmer Elf
He couldn't even climb
Up to his shelf!

Draw a line from the elf to each picture that begins with the short e sound.

Write.

E e _ _ _ _ _ _ _ _ _ _

© Instructional Fair • TS Denison   65   IF87101 "Fun"damental Phonics

Page 66

A B C Read the poem.

Name _____

Circle each letter i that is making a short i sound.

In an Instant

In an instant,
An inchworm inches near.
In an instant,
I can disappear!

Color each picture on the inchworm that begins with the short i sound.

© Instructional Fair • TS Denison   66   IF87101 "Fun"damental Phonics

© Instructional Fair • TS Denison   IF87101 "Fun"damental Phonics

short-vowel sounds: /o/

Read the poem.

Circle each letter *o* that is making a short *o* sound.

Otter
Otter likes to play
With many things
Like olives, octagons,
And big, round rings.

Otter only thinks about things that begin with the short *o* sound. Circle each picture that starts with the sound of short *o*.

Write. _____

© Instructional Fair • TS Denison   IF87101 *"Fun"damental Phonics*

Page 67

---

short-vowel sounds: /u/

Read the poem.

Circle each letter *u* that is making a short *u* sound.

Umbrellas Up
An umbrella goes up,
An umbrella goes down.
People hide under umbrellas
All over town.

Write *U u* on the lines on each umbrella. Then draw a line from each umbrella to a picture that starts with the short *u* sound.

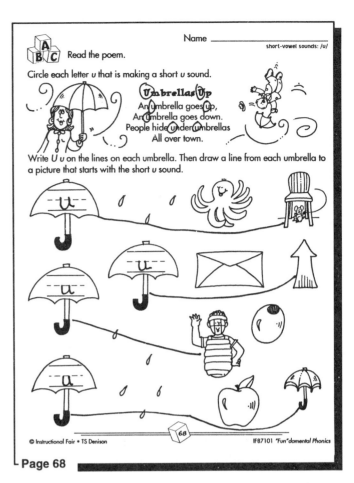

© Instructional Fair • TS Denison   IF87101 *"Fun"damental Phonics*

Page 68

---

long-vowel sounds: /a/

Read the poem.

Circle each letter *a* that is making a long *a* sound.

Amy and Kate
On a day rainy and gray,
Amy and Kate stay inside to play.
They wear aprons to paint,
They shape some clay,
Until the rain goes away.

Here are pictures that Amy and Kate painted! Color the pictures that start with the sound of long *a*.

Write. _____

© Instructional Fair • TS Denison   IF87101 *"Fun"damental Phonics*

Page 69

---

long-vowel sounds: /e/

Read the poem.

Circle each letter *e* that is making a long *e* sound.

Easel Art
Paint a picture
On an easel
Of a single bee.
Or paint two or three
By a leafy tree.

Use a green crayon to draw a circle around the pictures that start with the long *e* sound.

Write. _____

© Instructional Fair • TS Denison   IF87101 *"Fun"damental Phonics*

Page 70

© Instructional Fair • TS Denison   IF87101 *"Fun"damental Phonics*

Page 71

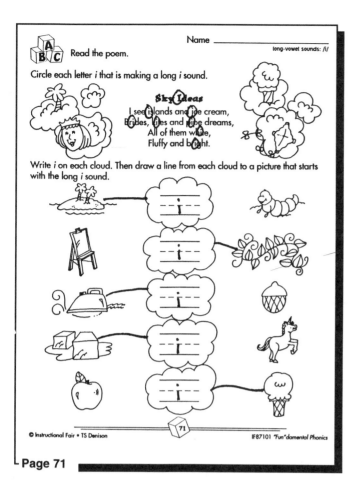

long-vowel sounds: /i/

A B C Read the poem.

Circle each letter *i* that is making a long *i* sound.

Sky Ideas
I see islands and ice cream,
Brides, ties and ripe dreams,
All of them white,
Fluffy and bright.

Write *i* on each cloud. Then draw a line from each cloud to a picture that starts with the long *i* sound.

i *i* *i* *i* *i*

© Instructional Fair • TS Denison   71   IF87101 *"Fun"damental Phonics*

Page 72

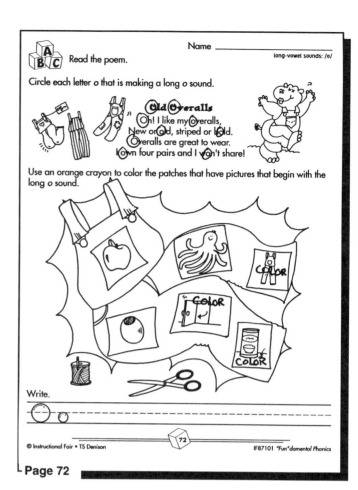

long-vowel sounds: /o/

A B C Read the poem.

Circle each letter *o* that is making a long *o* sound.

Old Overalls
Oh! I like my overalls,
New or old, striped or bold.
Overalls are great to wear.
I own four pairs and I won't share!

Use an orange crayon to color the patches that have pictures that begin with the long *o* sound.

COLOR   COLOR   COLOR

Write.
_____

© Instructional Fair • TS Denison   72   IF87101 *"Fun"damental Phonics*

Page 73

long-vowel sounds: /u/

A B C Read the poem.

Circle each letter *u* that is making a long *u* sound.

Unique
Use a rocket
To fly up high
Through the bright and starry sky.
In all the universe,
You are unique,
Like each star and place
That astronauts seek.

Draw a line from the unicorn to the pictures that start with the long *u* sound.

Write.
_u_____

© Instructional Fair • TS Denison   73   IF87101 *"Fun"damental Phonics*

Page 74

consonant blends: /bl/

A B C Read the poem.

Circle the two letters that make the sound you hear at the beginning of 🏠

Blizzard
Blizzard blowing
On our block!
Blow! Blow!
Blasts of snow!

Find your way through the blowing blizzard. Take the path with the pictures that begin with the sound of *bl*.

2 + 2

Write.
_bl_____

© Instructional Fair • TS Denison   74   IF87101 *"Fun"damental Phonics*

IF87101 *"Fun"damental Phonics*

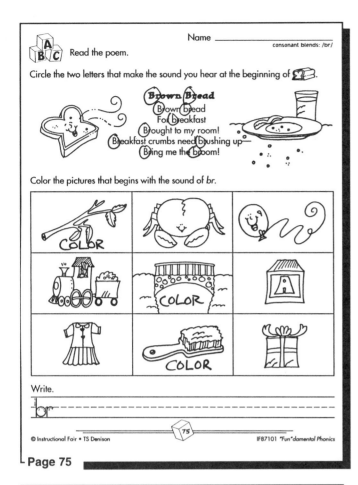

Name _____

A B C Read the poem.

Circle the two letters that make the sound you hear at the beginning of 🍞.

Brown Bread
Brown bread
For breakfast
Brought to my room!
Breakfast crumbs need brushing up—
Bring me the broom!

Color the pictures that begins with the sound of *br*.

Write.
br

© Instructional Fair • TS Denison   75   IF87101 *"Fun"damental Phonics*

Page 75

Name _____

A B C Read the poem.

Circle the two letters that make the sound you hear at the beginning of ☁.

Clean the Clouds
Climb up
And clean these clouds!
We can't see up here.
Take a cloth
And clean up close
Until each cloud is clear!

Color each cloud with a picture that begins with the sound of *cl*.

Write.
cl

© Instructional Fair • TS Denison   76   IF87101 *"Fun"damental Phonics*

Page 76

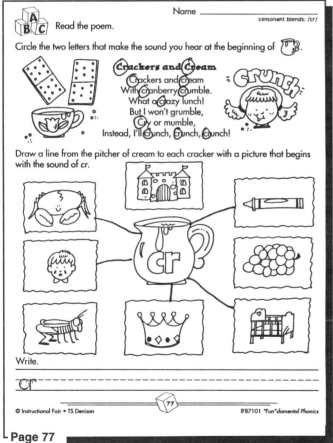

Name _____

A B C Read the poem.

Circle the two letters that make the sound you hear at the beginning of 🫖.

Crackers and Cream
Crackers and cream
With cranberry crumble.
What a crazy lunch!
But I won't grumble,
Cry or mumble,
Instead, I'll crunch, crunch, crunch!

CRUNCH

Draw a line from the pitcher of cream to each cracker with a picture that begins with the sound of *cr*.

cr

Write.
cr

© Instructional Fair • TS Denison   77   IF87101 *"Fun"damental Phonics*

Page 77

Name _____

A B C Read the poem.

Circle the two letters that make the sound you hear at the beginning of 🐉.

Dragon Dream
A dragon is drinking
From the dripping drain.
Now it's dragging
My dresser drawer!
It's drumming my drum,
It's drying a dress—
Oh, dear! I'm dreaming some more!

Circle the pictures that begin with the sound of *dr*.

Write.
dr

© Instructional Fair • TS Denison   78   IF87101 *"Fun"damental Phonics*

Page 78

123

© Instructional Fair • TS Denison   IF87101 *"Fun"damental Phonics*

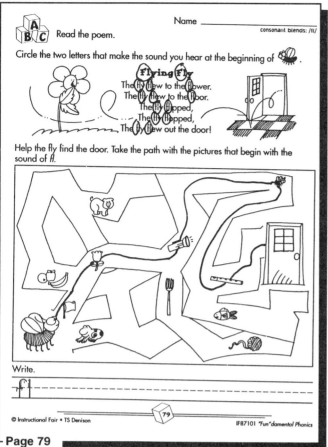

A B C Read the poem.

Name _____

Circle the two letters that make the sound you hear at the beginning of 🦟.

Flying fly
The fly flew to the flower.
The fly flew to the floor.
The fly flopped,
The fly flopped,
The fly flew out the door!

Help the fly find the door. Take the path with the pictures that begin with the sound of *fl*.

Write.

fl _____

79

© Instructional Fair • TS Denison   IF87101 *"Fun"damental Phonics*

Page 79

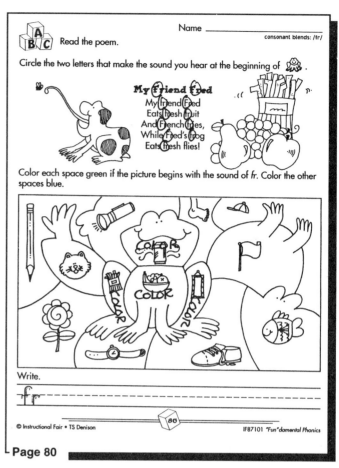

A B C Read the poem.

Name _____

Circle the two letters that make the sound you hear at the beginning of 🐸.

My friend Fred
My friend Fred
Eats fresh fruit
And French fries,
While Fred's frog
Eats fresh flies!

Color each space green if the picture begins with the sound of *fr*. Color the other spaces blue.

Write.

fr _____

80

© Instructional Fair • TS Denison   IF87101 *"Fun"damental Phonics*

Page 80

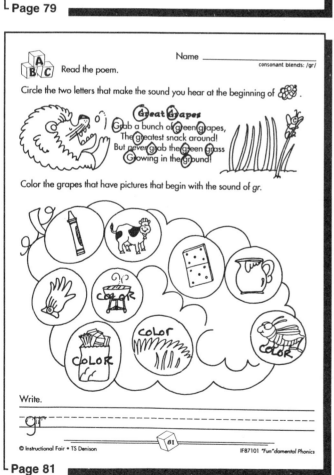

A B C Read the poem.

Name _____

Circle the two letters that make the sound you hear at the beginning of 🍇.

Great Grapes
Grab a bunch of green grapes,
The greatest snack around!
But never grab the green grass
Growing in the ground!

Color the grapes that have pictures that begin with the sound of *gr*.

Write.

gr _____

81

© Instructional Fair • TS Denison   IF87101 *"Fun"damental Phonics*

Page 81

A B C Read the poem.

Name _____

Circle the two letters that make the sound you hear at the beginning of 🎖️.

Pretending
Let's pretend
We're prince and princess,
Very proud and pretty.
People will praise us,
Present us with prizes
As we protect our city!

Write *pr* on the lines below the pictures that begin with the sound of *pr*.

_____   _____   _____

_____   *pr*   _____

pr   _____   *pr*

Write.

pr _____

82

© Instructional Fair • TS Denison   IF87101 *"Fun"damental Phonics*

Page 82

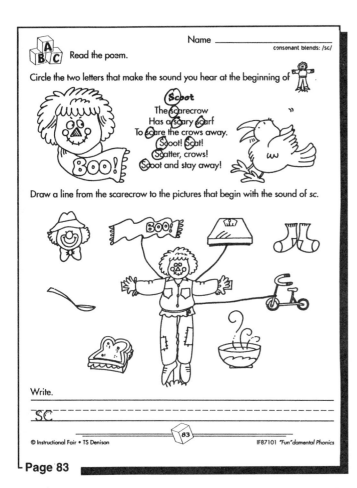

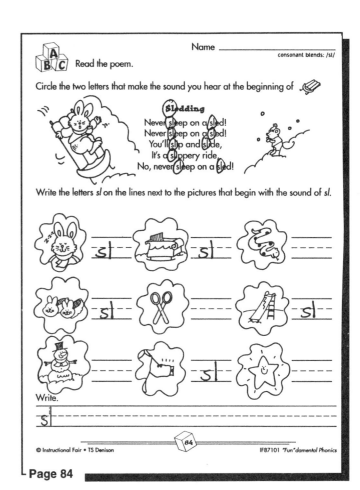

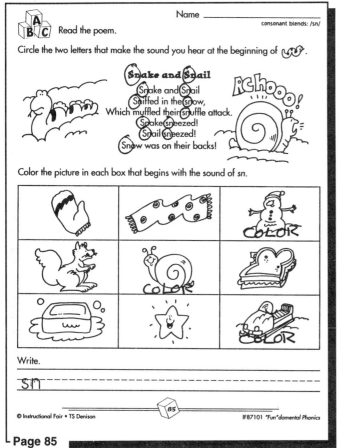

© Instructional Fair • TS Denison

IF87101 "Fun"damental Phonics

Page 87

Read the poem.

Circle the two letters that make the sound you hear at the beginning of [stop sign].

Stop!
Stop! Don't step up!
Stay put! Stand still!
Sticks and stones
Are on those stairs.
You may start to
Stumble there!

Color each stone that has a picture that begins with the sound of *st*.

Write.

s t _____

© Instructional Fair • TS Denison   87   IF87101 "Fun"damental Phonics

Page 88

Read the poem.

Circle the two letters that make the sound you hear at the beginning of [swan].

Swimming Swan
A swimming swan
Is swift and sweet,
So sweet it sweeps me
Off my feet!

Draw a line from the swan to each word that begins with the sound of *sw*.

Write.

s w _____

© Instructional Fair • TS Denison   88   IF87101 "Fun"damental Phonics

Page 89

Read the poem.

Circle the two letters that make the sound you hear at the beginning of [train].

Travel by Train
Travel by train!
The trip is a treat.
When trucks and trailers
Are trapped in traffic,
Train tracks can't be beat.

Take a train ride! Color the pictures that begin with the sound of *tr*.

Write.

t r _____

© Instructional Fair • TS Denison   89   IF87101 "Fun"damental Phonics

Page 90

Read the poem.

Circle the words that end in *ap*.

Clap and Tap
Hands clap!
Arms flap!
Fingers snap!
Feet tap!
Knuckles rap!

Read each sentence and look at the picture clue. Write the *ap* word on each line. Then write that word in its numbered space in the puzzle.

1. I had a   cap
2. Look at the   map
3. The baby took a   nap
4. Look at the mouse   trap
5. My fingers   snap
6. I can   clap

© Instructional Fair • TS Denison   90   IF87101 "Fun"damental Phonics

IF87101 "Fun"damental Phonics

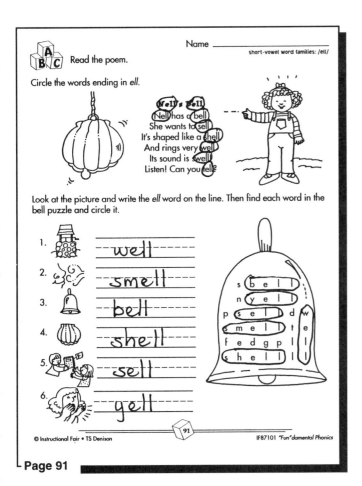

Page 91

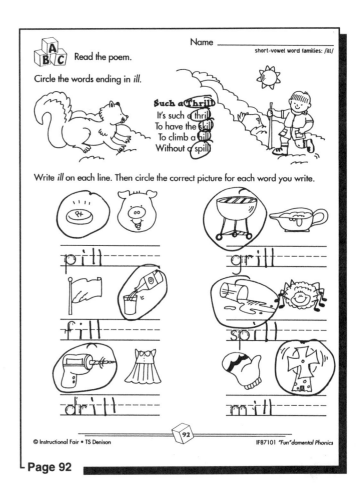

Page 92

Page 93

Page 94

IF87101 *"Fun"damental Phonics*

Read the poem.

long-vowel word families: /ake/

Circle the words ending in *ake*.

Don't Shake a Snake
Never use a rake
To give a snake a shake
Just to see it's awake!
For goodness sake!

Write the word on the lines under each
picture. Use the Word Bank to help you.
Then find and circle the words in the puzzle.

Word Bank
snake   lake   flake
cake   rake   bake

bake   cake   flake

snake   rake   lake

a	b	a	k	e	s	r	a	k	e	r
s	n	a	k	e	c	a	k	e	k	e
k	c	a	k	e	e	f	l	a	k	e

© Instructional Fair • TS Denison   95   IF87101 *"Fun"damental Phonics*

Page 95

Read the poem.

long-vowel word families: /eat/

Circle the words ending in *eat*.

Wheat
What is wheat?
It is grain, not meat
Tall and gold in the summer heat
Cutting it is quite a feat!
Then it's baked into the bread we eat.

Write the word on the lines under each
picture. Use the Word Bank to help you.
Find and circle the words in the puzzle.

Word Bank
seat   beat   meat
pleat   heat   eat

eat   meat   pleat

heat   seat   beat

j	d	b	e	a	t	v	c	p	a	b	l	n
e	m	b	r	y	e	a	g	y	h	e	a	t
a	s	d	a	p	l	e	a	t	l	g	e	o
t	z	m	e	a	t	e	m	c	a	e	w	f
b	f	e	h	k	t	b	t	s	e	a	t	s

© Instructional Fair • TS Denison   96   IF87101 *"Fun"damental Phonics*

Page 96

Read the poem.

long-vowel word families: /ide/

Circle the words ending in *ide*.

Slide Ride
Let's both glide
Down the slide outside.
It's tall and wide
For a fast, wild ride!

Write the word below each picture. Use
the Word Bank to help you. Then find and
circle the words in the puzzle.

Word Bank
slide   side   ride
bride   hide   inside

ride   hide

slide   inside

side   bride

© Instructional Fair • TS Denison   97   IF87101 *"Fun"damental Phonics*

Page 97

Read the poem.

long-vowel word families: /oat/

Circle the words ending in *oat*.

Silly Goat
A silly goat
Jumped off a boat
To swim and float
He had no coat
Though he loved to float,
He got a sore throat!

Write the word for each picture on the
lines. Use the Word Bank to help you.
Then write the words in the puzzle.

Word Bank
goat   boat   float
coat   moat   oat

Across
3. Float
4. moat
6. goat

Down
1. boat
2. coat
5. oat

© Instructional Fair • TS Denison   98   IF87101 *"Fun"damental Phonics*

Page 98

© Instructional Fair • TS Denison

128

IF87101 *"Fun"damental Phonics*